The Peddler Of Hearts: A Play For Young People

Gertrude Knevels

In the interest of creating a more extensive selection of rare historical book reprints, we have chosen to reproduce this title even though it may possibly have occasional imperfections such as missing and blurred pages, missing text, poor pictures, markings, dark backgrounds and other reproduction issues beyond our control. Because this work is culturally important, we have made it available as a part of our commitment to protecting, preserving and promoting the world's literature. Thank you for your understanding.

The Peddler of Hearts

A Play for Young People

By
GERTRUDE KNEVELS

Complete with Songs, Dances and
Selected Music

BOSTON
WALTER H. BAKER & CO.
1917

The Peddler of Hearts

CHARACTERS

THE PRINCE OF HERZIMWALD.
BURGOMASTER OF HERZIMWALD.
A COBBLER.
THE BUTCHER.
THE BAKER.
THE CANDLESTICK-MAKER.
THE BUTCHER'S WIFE.
THE BAKER'S WIFE.
THE CANDLESTICK-MAKER'S WIFE.
BELROSE, *the Burgomaster's daughter.*
GRETEL, *the Goose-girl.*
RUDOLF, *her lover.*
KARL, *first boy.*
FIVE OTHER BOYS.
HILDA, *first girl.*
FIVE OTHER GIRLS.
SIX ELVES, *Toadkin, Teaser, Pincher, Snatch, Sneak and Moss Face.*
THE ELF-KING, *or Peddler of Hearts.*

COPYRIGHT, 1917, BY GERTRUDE KNEVELS
Free for amateur performance.   Professional stage-right reserved.

COSTUMES

PRINCE. Long cloak over slashed tunic. Short puffed trousers, long stockings and low buckled shoes. Lace ruffles at sleeves and lace collar. A flat velvet cap with a white feather, sword, and gold chain about neck.

BURGOMASTER. Broad, low-crowned black hat. Deep white collars and cuffs. Long-tailed brown or crimson coat and knee-breeches. Thick gold chain about neck. Low buckled shoes.

BUTCHER, BAKER, CANDLESTICK-MAKER and COBBLER. Peasant smocks over knee-breeches, white stockings and low black shoes. Butcher and Baker have white caps and aprons. Candlestick-Maker carries bag of tools and bundle of wicks and moulds. Butcher wears string of imitation sausages round his neck, and when quarrelsome can use a ham as a weapon. Baker fights with a long loaf of bread which he wields as a boy does a baseball bat. Cobbler wears a leather apron and plays a fiddle. Where the music is furnished by an orchestra, he can use an imitation instrument.

WOMEN. Peasant costumes in subdued colors. Dark skirts, white blouses, bodices black or in contrasting colors. Embroidered aprons. Peasant caps. Baker's wife is oldest, Butcher's wife is very fat.

GIRLS. Peasant costumes in bright colors. Skirts with stripes of contrasting color. Black velvet bodices, white blouses and aprons, pretty winged caps. Buckled shoes. On first entrance all carry garlands and bunches of flowers, also loose flowers in aprons. Hair in long braids.

GRETEL. A ragged brown dress, short sleeved and low necked, hair flowing, wooden shoes or bare feet. On first entrance carries basket containing primrose cross. Second entrance carries gooseherds' wand, a slender forked stick. Third entrance assists Rudolf to carry pack of hearts.

BOYS. Peasant costume. White blouses, bright colored vests, short trousers. Peasant hats. White stockings, buckled shoes.

BELROSE. A short-waisted, full-skirted dress with pointed bodice of pale blue brocaded with gold. A very good effect for this dress at a small cost can be obtained by using blue satine and stitching on figures cut from gold paper. A white mantle or train, lined with blue and bordered with gold tinsel braid. A high, cornucopia-shaped head-dress of white or gold with a pale blue veil falling from the point down wearer's back. Blue or gilt shoes. Hair worn in long curls or braids drawn forward.

ELVES. Long-sleeved tunics of brown or green cambric. Toadkin should dress in brown. Edges of sleeves and bottoms of tunics not hemmed but fringed or cut in points. Short trousers finished in same way. High pointed green or scarlet caps. No shoes but stockings to match suits having toes capped with same colored cloth wired out in long sharp points.

ELF-KING. Scarlet suit somewhat on order of Jester's costume, a picture of which can be found in any library. A pointed cap with long feather. Carries a brown sackcloth pack full of false hearts. These hearts are cut from cardboard and covered with red, blue, gold or silver paper. The special heart reserved for Belrose should be wound with Christmas tinsel.

STORY OF THE PLAY

Because Mortals have dared to build within the borders of the elfin wood, wicked elves have laid a curse upon the Village of Herzimwald. On the town's happiest day, the day of the betrothal of the Burgomaster's beautiful daughter to the young Prince, the Elf-King, disguised as a Peddler of Hearts, arrives in the marketplace. He tricks the people into exchanging their good flesh-and-blood hearts for the gilded baubles he sells them. Now the Prince comes to find his beloved bewitched, and the holiday jollity of the town changed to mourning. In place of the kindly mirth for which the village has ever been famous, there is quarreling, discord, misery. The Prince's well-meant efforts to the succor of the people are unsuccessful, and it is only by the unselfishness of the little Goose-Girl—who "had never a penny to buy her a new heart"—and through the courage of her boy lover, that the hearts are finally restored. The people of Herzimwald, happy once more, promise hereafter to "Seek only the true gold!"

The Peddler of Hearts

ACT I

SCENE 1.—*Market-place in village of Herzimwald. Time, morning. Gaily decorated booths of* BUTCHER, BAKER *and* CANDLESTICK-MAKER *up* C., *and at* R. *and* L.

(BUTCH., BAK., *and* C.-M., *with their wives, are busily arranging goods on counters.* COBBLER *sits on bench beside a pile of old shoes, playing his fiddle and singing. Others gradually stop work to listen, joining in on last verse; then, as if unable to resist any longer, they pair off and dance. See Appendix for the Description of Dances and Music.*)

COB. (*singing*).
    Ha, ha, ha, and ho, ho, ho!
      Life is full of sunshine, so
    As along my way I go,
      I must laugh—ho, ho! ho, ho!

    Laughing, chaffing, that suits me,
      My light heart from care is free,
    So the joke I always see —
      Yes, oh, yes, a joke suits me!

    Blue's the color for my sky,
      What if clouds go sailing by?
    Silver linings I can spy —
      In my happy, happy sky!

ALL (*joining in*).
    Ha, ha, ha, and ho, ho, ho!
      Life is full of sunshine, so —
    As along my way I go,
      I must laugh, ho, ho! ho, ho!

BUTCHER'S WIFE (*puffing and panting at end of dance*). There, stop, not another step! I'm too fat——

C.-M. (*her partner*). One more turn—just one! Remember what day this is.

BUTCH. 'Tisn't every day our Burgomaster's daughter gets herself betrothed to a Prince!

BAK. 'Tisn't every day a Prince has the luck to meet so sweet a maid as our Belrose. Here's joy to her! (*Waves cap.*) Belrose the Beautiful! Belrose——

BAKER'S WIFE. There, there, husband, that will do! Belrose is a good girl, but that pretty head of hers will likely be turned now 'tis to wear a crown. Come, Karl, get to work! Do you want the Prince to find us in such a mess as this?

(*Goes to booth and begins to arrange goods. Other women follow her example, but men continue to take their ease.*)

BAK. (*seating himself deliberately and lighting pipe*). Time enough! Time a-plenty!

BUTCH. 'Tis half a day's journey from the Palace. He'll not be here before noon.

CANDLESTICK-MAKER'S WIFE. There's a deal to be done before that.

C.-M. Right you are, Katrinka. Still, it does us old folks good to have a bit of fun now and then. I never was one for pulling a long face myself.

BAK. Nor I. Long faces aren't the style in Herzimwald, and never have been. Why, from our great-grandfather's times down to this very day, we hold the reputation of being the maddest, merriest folk in all the countryside. Now, I wonder——

BAK.'S WIFE (*interrupting*). I wonder how long 'twill be before we change our tune!

BUTCH.'S WIFE. Change our tune?

BAK.'S WIFE. Aye—for change it we must, if ever the old tale comes true.

C.-M.'S WIFE. What tale is that?

BAK.'S WIFE. Do you mean to say you've never heard it? Many's the winter night beside the fire my old Granny used to tell us children the story—how because our town was built on the edge of the elves' wood, the elves have laid a curse on it.

BUTCH.'S WIFE (*shuddering and looking over shoulder*). Elves! Hush, don't speak of them to-day; it might bring bad luck!

BUTCH. Tush! What nonsense!

COB. Seems to me now I do remember some old rhyme my mother used to sing to me, when I was a little chap so high——

BAK.'S WIFE (*eagerly*). Did it go like this? (*Recites.*)

> Herzimwald, so gay, so good,
> Built within the Elf-King's wood,
> Some day sorrow shalt thou know,
> Some day elves shall bring thee woe—
> Till a merry-hearted maid
> Goes alone to Elf-King's glade!

BAK. Nonsense, old women's nonsense! Nobody could make head or tail of such stuff.

BUTCH. As if anybody feared elves nowadays!

BAK.'S WIFE (*turning on both*). Nonsense, is it? And you don't fear the elves, Hans Fleischmann? Oh, no! Then tell me why it is not one of you men dares go alone into the forest? My son Rudolf's the only one who's not afraid, though he is but a lad.

BUTCH. I'll not say a stray elf isn't seen now and then——

BUTCH.'S WIFE (*clapping hand over his mouth*). Hush! Didn't I tell you not to speak of them? Do you want to scare the girls? Here they come now with their garlands for the Prince's arch.

(*Music. See Appendix.*)

Enter HILDA *and other girls carrying garlands of flowers. Some have loose flowers in aprons. They dance, older people watching approvingly and afterward applauding.*

COB. Very fine! Very pretty! So that's the way you'll dance to-night before the Prince—eh?

HILDA. Yes, that's the way! Don't we know our steps nicely? And—see, these are our garlands for the Prince's arch. But we must have wreaths, girls; one for his Highness and one for our Belrose. Who will make them?

2D GIRL. Gretel the Goose-girl makes the prettiest wreaths of any girl in the town.

3D GIRL. But Gretel's gone to look for primroses!

4TH GIRL (*standing on bench to loop daisy chain across booth*). Primroses? It's lilies and roses we ought to have to-day!

2D GIRL. We need some green branches.
5TH GIRL. The boys are bringing them.

(COB. *goes to meet* BOYS, *returning with them.*)

4TH GIRL. Here they come!
HILDA. Sh! Let's not notice them!
5TH GIRL. Let's pretend to be working!

(GIRLS *sit on ground in two groups at* R. *and* L., *bending over flowers.* BOYS *march in, whistling merrily and headed by* COB. *playing his fiddle.* BOYS *carry green branches. They drop these, pull* GIRLS *to feet, and make them dance. See Description of Dances and Music. Older people in background applaud, then, baskets in hand, bustle off stage as if going for merchandise.* COB. *follows.*)

HILDA (*pulling away from her partner*). Oh, Karl, but you're clumsy! If Rudolf were here, I wouldn't be dancing with you!
GIRLS. Where's Rudolf? We want Rudolf!
KARL. Oh, he's hard at work in the forest.
2D BOY. Working? But to-day's a holiday!
KARL. Rudolf doesn't want a holiday. He's splitting logs to build a house.
3D BOY. Perhaps he's going to follow the Prince's example!
KARL. They say he's picked his sweetheart.
GIRLS. His sweetheart?
KARL. Oh, it's not you, Hilda, you needn't fall a-blushing!
HILDA. How dare you say I'm blushing?

(*She chases him across stage and boxes his ears.*)

2D GIRL (*looking off*). Why, here comes Rudolf now! And who do you think is with him?
GIRLS. Who?
2D GIRL. Gretel, the Goose-girl!

Enter RUDOLF *and* GRETEL, *hand in hand.* RUD. *carries an axe over his shoulder,* GRE. *a little basket.* BOYS *and* GIRLS *surround them teasingly.*

BOYS.
GIRLS. } Rudolf, Rudolf; tell us who's your sweetheart?
HILDA (*tossing him a flower*). I dare you to give her this!
RUD. (*catching it*). I thank you!

(*He bows, gives flower to* GRE. *who tucks it in her belt and bobs him a curtsey.*)

GIRLS } (*taking hands and dancing merrily round couple*).
BOYS

    Gretel and Rudolf, ho, ho! ho, ho!
    Gretel and Rudolf, ho, *ho!*

RUD. (*breaking through circle*). There, girls, let me go. I only turned back with Gretel here, who had wandered too far after her primroses, and now I must get back to my work. To-night I'll spend with my good uncle who lives t'other side of the forest, but I'll be home again before to-morrow evening. (GIRLS *and* BOYS *turn aside to work on garlands.* KARL *runs out, whistling.* RUD. *draws* GRE. *down* C.) You'll promise me not to wander so far into the forest again, won't you, Gretel? I'm not afraid of the elves for myself, but for you——

GRE. But I fear for you, Rudolf! It was for you I wanted the primroses. Don't you know that they are holy flowers? A cross woven of primroses will keep off evil spirits. Take this, and keep it always about you. (*Gives him cross.*)

RUD. I will, little sweetheart, and thank you kindly. Good-bye!

GRE. Good-bye!

GIRLS. } Good-bye, Rudolf! Good luck to you!
BOYS.

(RUD. *runs off* L.)

Enter KARL.

KARL. Guess who's coming down the road!
BOYS. The Prince!
HILDA. And our wreaths not finished!
2D GIRL. Oh, my hair!
3D GIRL. And I'm not dressed!
KARL. Sillies, it's not the Prince at all, it's a peddler!
GIRLS (*disappointed*). Oh—nothing but a peddler!
KARL (*mysteriously*). But wait till you see him—the queerest chap I ever laid eyes on. He's got a yellow face and eyes as black as a hawk and a great big pack on his back, and he's dressed in scarlet with shiny things hung all over him. Yes, and he's singing as he comes. Listen!

(*All listen. Elfin music begins faintly and* ELF-KING'*s voice is heard singing outside.*)

HILDA. What fun! 'Twill serve to pass the time till the Prince comes. Let's run and meet him.

(GIRLS *and* BOYS *run out* L. *as older people come in from* R.)

BUTCH.'S WIFE. Did you hear that? What a queer tune!
BAK.'S WIFE (*frightened*). Don't listen—that's a bad tune—that's elf-music! Don't listen, I say!

(*Claps hands over own ears, but removes them almost immediately, listening with all her might.*)

BAK. Nonsense, wife! Why, 'tis nothing but a peddler. See, here's the fellow now!

(*Enter* KING, *dressed as* PEDDLER OF HEARTS, *dancing and singing.* BOYS *and* GIRLS *follow him in. All surround him admiringly.*)

PED. (*singing*).

    Hey ding-a-ding, a-ding!
    Hearts on a string, a string,
    Hey ding-a-ding, a-ding,
    Hearts on a string!
    Silver hearts, gold hearts,
    New hearts for old hearts,
    Come and buy new hearts,
    Hey ding-a-ding!

    Hey ding-a-ding, a-ding!
    Hearts on a string, a string,
    Hey ding-a-ding, a-ding,
    Hearts on a string!
    Red hearts and blue hearts,
    Bold hearts and true hearts,
    Come and buy new hearts,
    Hey ding-a-ding!

(*As he sings, the* PED. *turns round and round to display bright tinsel hearts on ribbon about his neck and showing from mouth of pack.*)

GRE. Whatever can he mean?

BAK. Your goods, fellow, what are your goods?

PED. (*in the voice of the hawker*). Hearts, hearts, who'll buy them? Hearts, hearts, who'll try them? Get rid of your old hearts, your cold hearts, your crusty, musty, dusty, work-a-day hearts! I give away hearts! Here are new hearts, red and blue hearts, fine and true hearts! All for you—hearts! Hearts! Silver and gold—new hearts for old!

(*While chanting, the* PED. *makes his way between the people to booth up* C., *takes place behind counter, and pours out a stream of hearts from pack. People crowd round, bringing out purses and counting money.*)

PEOPLE. How much? How much?

PED. Such a low price it is open to any one! Just your old heart and one silver penny—one!

(*All except* GRE., *the* BAK.'S WIFE, *and the* BUTCH.'S WIFE *scramble to buy the false hearts. All push and shove one another out of the way, but laughingly and in perfect good nature. As* PED. *receives money he hands each person a heart, and touches the heart of the buyer. The false hearts are slipped into vest-pockets of men and boys, and into kerchiefs of women and girls. The effect of the enchantment should be shown immediately in the expression and actions of buyers; gayety giving way to dull misery, kindliness to quarreling, etc.*)

GRE. Oh, dear, oh, dear, I never knew before 'twas so dreadful to be poor! If I only had a penny!

(*She darts into crowd, trying to borrow from one after another, but always being refused.*)

BAK.'S WIFE (*dragging her husband by his coat-tail out of crowd*). Come away, Karl, dear, come away! I wouldn't give up my good old heart, not for any new one!

BAK. (*who has just pocketed false heart, turning on her roughly*). Your good heart? You old scold, you ugly, silly shrew! You need a new heart, if any one does!

BAK.'S WIFE (*amazed*). Why, Karl, whatever is the matter with you? You never in all your life spoke like that to me before!

BUTCH.'S WIFE (*who has been making observations over shoulders of crowd*). Come along, Lotta, come along!

BAK.'s WIFE. No, no, I'm afraid! There's magic in this, magic I tell you. And yet—and yet—he said I needed a new heart!

BUTCH.'s WIFE. It doesn't seem to hurt at all. He just lays his hand on your old heart—so (*touching friend's heart*) and—pop—'tis gone! And you've a fine shiny new one in its place all red or gilt or silver! Come—we don't want to be behind the fashion!

(*She drags* BAK.'s WIFE *toward* PED. *Both purchase hearts.*)

C.-M.'s WIFE (*elbowing her way down* C.). Get out of my way there, will you? (*She roughly pushes* COB. *aside.*) See! I've the finest in the pack!

COB. (*returning shove*). Mine's a dozen times finer than yours, woman! Gilt and scarlet 'tis, with a pattern all of twisting silver snakes!

C.-M.'s WIFE. 'Tis not so heavy as mine!

COB. (*groaning*). Heavy? 'Tis the heaviest heart in the world!

HILDA (*thrusting herself between them*). Stupids! Is it likely any of us poor folk will get the finest? That's being saved for Belrose—(*sneering*) Belrose, the Prince's Bride!

GRE. (*delighted*). Here comes our pretty Belrose now! And the Burgomaster—he's always kind! Maybe he'll give me a penny!

Enter BELROSE *and* BURGOMASTER OF HERZIMWALD, *he pompous and kindly, she gay and smiling. She nods and kisses hands to* BOYS *and* GIRLS, *none of whom, except* GRE., *make any response, as all except* GOOSE-GIRL *have now received false hearts and the enchantment is beginning to be felt.*

BEL. Good-day to you, dear friends, good-day!

BURG. (*to* PED.). Well, well, fellow, what have you there?

PED. (*bowing and smirking as he approaches* BEL.). Best in my pack, I have laid it aside. See, a bright heart for the Prince's Bride! Solid gold, heavy and cold!

(*Displays golden heart.*)

BEL. Oh, oh, 'tis beautiful! And how it shines! I must have it—I must!

BURG. (*taking out fat purse*). Of course you shall. My girl must have the best of everything.

(*Gives* PED. *handful of money.*)

BEL. (*delighted*). Quick, be quick! But oh (*shrinking*), my old heart?
PED. (*speaking slowly and impressively as he lays hand on her heart*). Never again, never again, shall this cold heart feel joy or pain!
BEL. (*impatiently*). The new one, the new one!

(*She snatches new heart, slips it into bodice, and turns aside to gloat over treasure.*)

BURG. And now for myself. Have you anything more expensive?

(*While he bargains with* PED. *for last heart but one on string,* GRE., *who has tried in vain to attract* BURG.'S *attention, comes pouting down* C.)

GRE. 'Tis a shame! Nobody will lend me a penny! Oh dear, oh dear, if Rudolf were here, he would buy me that last little tinsel heart!
PED. (*slyly approaching her*). Give me your little sweet heart so true, and here, without price, is my last for you!
GRE. Oh, sir, thank you! (*She goes toward him eagerly, then draws back.*) But no, that wouldn't be honest! I don't want your goods if I can't pay! (*She looks at him closely.*) And after all, I don't believe—I don't believe I do want your heart! (*Starts back suddenly.*) Oh—I'm afraid, afraid!

(PED. *tries to grasp her and twist ribbon with heart about her neck, but she eludes him.* PED. *laughs, bows mockingly, takes sack, and slips away through crowd, all of whom by this time are too much occupied with their own misery to notice his going. At exit he stops a moment to gloat over them all, laughs loud and exultantly, waves mocking salute, and goes. Discord shows itself among people.*)

BAK. (*to wife*). Out of my sight! Off with you!

(*Threatens her.*)

BAK.'s WIFE. Be still!

BUTCH.'s WIFE (*to* BUTCH.). You trod on my foot, I say——

BUTCH. I don't care if I did. I don't care. I don't care for anything!

C.-M. Who pushed me? (*Turns on* COB.)

COB. Stand out of my way, or I'll pull your nose off!

GRE. Why, whatever is the matter with everybody?

BUTCH. (*putting her roughly aside*). Out of the way, Goose-girl! Back to your geese! A nice sight you are for the Prince to see, with your old brown dress and your ugly wooden shoes!

BURG. (*starting up as if from a dream*). The Prince! He may be here at any moment—and I'd forgotten he was coming. (*Turns angrily to daughter.*) Wake up, girl! (*Shakes her arm.*) Are you asleep? What's the matter with you? Have you forgotten the Prince is coming?

KARL. The Prince is here!

Enter PRINCE OF HERZIMWALD *hurriedly*.

PEOPLE (*echoing dully and without moving from places*). The Prince!

PRINCE (*looking about him in angry amazement*). So, my good people of Herzimwald, this is the welcome you give your Prince? A pleasant meeting, upon my word. A loyal greeting! (*Sees* BEL. *and springs to her side.*) Belrose, my beloved! (*Kneels and kisses her hand; she neither looks up nor moves.*) Have you no word for me? Child, what is it? Do you not know me? Speak! (*Feels her hands.*) Oh, she is cold—cold!

BAK.'s WIFE (*drearily*). She is bewitched. (*Looks round at people.*) We are all bewitched.

MEN } (*rousing suddenly in terror*). Aye, aye, be-
WOMEN } witched!

BURG. 'Twas the Peddler!

PEOPLE. Aye—the Peddler!

(*They shake fists angrily in direction taken by* PED.)

BAK.'s WIFE. Too late. He's gone—gone and left the curse behind.

PEOPLE. The curse has come on Herzimwald!

PRINCE (*to people*). Fools! What care I if the whole pack of you be bewitched and cursed together—were my sweet love but spared! (*Throws himself on knees beside* BEL.) Belrose, have you forgotten? This very day we were to be betrothed! Speak! Do you no longer love me?

BEL. (*raising head slowly, laying hand on heart, and using sad, dull voice*).

"Never again, never again
Shall this cold heart feel joy or pain!"

CURTAIN

SCENE 2.—*Same as Scene 1. Time, morning of day following* PED.'s *visit. Merchandise on booths, decorations hanging unfinished.*

(COB., C.-M., *his wife and other women sit about stage in dull, despairing attitudes. As curtain rises* BAK. *chases* BUTCH. *across stage, striking him with long loaf of bread.*)

BUTCH. Have done, won't you? Can't you let me alone? Can't you let a poor man alone to have a little comfort in his misery?

BAK. Be still, then. I'm sick of your moaning and your groaning. Do you think nobody's unhappy but yourself?

BUTCH. I know I'm the most miserable man in Herzimwald!

COB. (*springing to feet in sudden passion*). 'Tis a lie! I am! (*Flings a shoe at* BUTCH.)

BAK. (*whacking* COB. *with loaf*). No, no, I am!

(*As all glare at one another angrily,* PRINCE *enters hurriedly from* R.)

PRINCE. How now? Quarreling here too? I believe the old crone was right, the whole town's bewitched! Here, fellow. (*Beckons* BAK.) Come here, I say. (*Takes him by arm.*) Now listen to me ——

BAK. (*dolefully, fetching a long face*). Yes, your Highness!

PRINCE (*pointing*). Look up there now; don't you see the sun is shining?

Bak. (*still more dolefully*). Aye, your Highness, I see it. I see the sun a-shining; fit to bake the life out of a man! Drying up the pasture, parching the young wheat, taking the bread out of our very mouths. Oh, yes, deary-me, yes, your Highness, I see the sun a-shining!

Prince. But it's Springtime, man, it's Springtime! In the fields the buds are coming into bloom, in the woods the birds are singing fit to burst their hearts!

Cob. (*interrupting*). And here in Herzimwald we're sighing fit to burst ours. Oho! (*Sighs long and dismally.*)

People (*echoing*). Oho!

Prince (*releasing* Bak. *and turning on* Cob.). I tell you 'tis the time of year for folks to be merry, old men and young, wives and—(*he hesitates as* Bel. *enters, led between two of the girls and followed sadly by others*) wives and maidens! (*He goes to* Bel., *lifts her hand and kisses it, speaking gently as though to a sick child.*) Belrose! Belrose!

(*She does not seem to hear.* Prince *leads her to bench,* Girls *group behind her.*)

Bak.'s Wife (*coming down* c., *and speaking with bitter emphasis*). You see, your Highness, the old crone *was* right! The whole town's bewitched, and if you'd see on whom the curse has fallen heaviest, you have not far to look.

(*Points to* Bel. *and laughs maliciously.*)

C.-M.'s Wife. Belrose the Beautiful! Aye—she's beautiful now, with her heavy eyes and her face a yard long!

Butch.'s Wife. Belrose the Burgomaster's daughter! She must have the best in the pack. Ah, yes! The shining heart, the solid gold heart! (*Viciously.*) Ah! I hope 'twill weigh in her breast like a stone until she dies!

Prince (*to* Girls). Take her away! (Girls *lead* Bel. *out.* Prince *turns angrily on people.*) Shame on you all, I say. Shame on you all! Nothing have I heard this day in all this wretched town but moaning and groaning, quarreling and complaining. Are you all alike? Is there no hope? Not one bright face—one happy heart in this unhappy town?

(*Gay music heard outside. See Appendix.* Gre., *carrying a long, slender forked stick, dances in laughing. At first she does not see the* Prince.)

GRE. (*singing*).
>Ha, ha, ha, and ho, ho, ho!
>Life is full of sunshine, so—
>As along my way I go,
>I must laugh, ho, ho, ho, *ho !*

(*She ends song with joyful skip and hop, then runs to* COB. *and throws her arms round his neck.*) Oh, Peter Heel, Peter Heel, if you'll promise not to scold, I'll tell you something funny! The old gray goose is lost again; 'tis the third time since——

COB. (*pushing her away*). Silence, girl—the Prince——

GRE. Oh! (*Bobs courtesy.*) Give you good-day, your Highness!

PRINCE. Bravo, little one, bravo! I'll swear to it your heart came not out of the Peddler's pack!

GRE. No, Highness, for I had never a penny in the world, and nobody would lend me one!

PRINCE (*solemnly*). And well it was for you. You alone in all of Herzimwald, little Goose-girl, have escaped enchantment.

GRE. Enchantment? (*Points to people.*) Is that what's the matter with them?

PRINCE. Aye, so they say—magic!

BAK.'S WIFE. I told you so, I told you so. Magic, I said, wicked magic, elves' magic, but nobody would listen——

BAK. Who wants to listen to your clacking tongue? Be still, woman!

PRINCE. Let her speak.

BAK.'S WIFE (*importantly*). 'Twas but yesterday, your Highness, I was telling them of the curse——

PRINCE. The curse?

BAK.'S WIFE. Ay, the doom that's come upon us all—— (*Recites.*)

>Herzimwald, so gay, so good,
>Built within the Elf-King's wood,
>Some day sorrow shalt thou know,
>Some day elves shall bring thee woe,
>Till a merry-hearted maid
>Goes alone to Elf-King's glade!

COB. 'Tis the curse! We've waited for it all these years, and now 'tis come.

BAK. Blockhead, be still! I'll tell you something you could never guess, that peddler was——
BAK.'S WIFE. The Elf-King!
BAK.
COB. } Ay, the Elf-King himself!
PRINCE. Come, come, this is madness——
BAK. No, truth, your Highness. 'Twas he who robbed us of our good old hearts, our flesh-and-blood hearts, and left these fiendish lumps of gold and silver to weigh us down in sorrow to our graves. And there's no help!

(*He sighs mournfully.*)

PEOPLE. No help! No help!
PRINCE. I say there is! How went the rhyme? "Till a merry-hearted maid goes alone to Elf-King's glade——"
BAK.'S WIFE. But that would be the very heart of the forest, your Highness. Hardly a man in the town would dare venture so far, and what maid——
PRINCE. Gretel, the Goose-girl!
GRE. I? (*Runs to* PRINCE.) Oh, but your Highness, you don't mean you would send me?
PRINCE. I'll not send you, little Gretel, no! Here, on my knees (*bending his knee to her*), I beg you to go and save your people!

(*As* GRE. *hesitates, elfin music is faintly heard in distance.*)

BAK.'S WIFE. The music; the wicked elves' music! Do you hear? 'Tis calling her!
GRE. Yes, 'tis calling me. I hear! Farewell, your Highness! (*Kisses* PRINCE'S *hand.*) I am coming! I am coming!

(*Runs off* L. *Men look after her in terror. Women fall on knees and hide faces. Elfin music swells triumphantly.*)

CURTAIN

ACT II

SCENE 1.—*A glade in the* KING's *wood.*

(*The elves,* MOSS FACE, SNATCH, TEASER, PINCHER *and* SNEAK *are half-concealed behind stumps and bushes, as if lying in wait for some one.* TOADKIN *is keeping watch up* L. *Elfin music plays softly, then ceases abruptly as merry whistling is heard outside.* TOAD. *hides. Enter* RUD., *axe on shoulder. He stops whistling and stands looking uneasily about him.*)

RUD. Lordy, but it's still here! The stillest spot in all the forest! Even the birds seem to fear this place. At home in Mother's kitchen I laugh at tales of elves and their magic, but here, in these dark woods —— (*Nearest* ELF, *creeping from behind bush, makes a grab at* RUD.'s *ankle, then darts back to hiding.* RUD. *whirls round, striking vainly with axe.*) Oh, you would, would you? Take that! I know you're there, though I can't see you now. All day long you've been hunting me, sly little wretches that you are. Not that I care! (*He strikes again in vain as another* ELF *twitches his coat-tail.*) Pooh—no, indeed! Afraid of elves? Not I! (RUD.'s *manner indicates that, for all his brave words, his courage is beginning to fail. Elfin music begins again and* ELVES *begin to creep from hiding as if ready to pounce.*) And if I were, haven't I the holy primroses to protect me? (*As he takes primrose cross from pocket and holds it up, elf music ceases abruptly and* ELVES *shrink back.*) Gretel's primroses—bless her little kind heart! They'll keep me safe all the day long!

(*He shoulders axe, whistles gaily, and goes out at* L., *holding cross in plain sight.* ELVES *spring from hiding and gaze angrily after him.*)

PINCH. He's gone, he's gone! Your fault, Toadkin.
TOAD. (*hiding face*). Oh—primroses—they scorch my eyeballs!
MOSS. They burn my heart like little yellow flames.
TEAS. They smother me!

PINCH. (*solemnly*). And yet we know our King's command! Rudolf the Wood-cutter must roam the forest no more.

SNEAK. Shall we follow him?

TOAD. No, no; wait till it's dark!

MOSS. But the little yellow flames will burn more brightly then!

PINCH. We won't mind then. We'll have him!

SNEAK. What shall we do to him?

PINCH. Pinch him!

MOSS. Scratch his eyes out!

SNATCH. Jump on his back, dig in our claws, and ride him till he drops!

TOAD. (*leaping for joy*). Hey, hey, what fun! Ho, ho!

PINCH. (*grabbing* TOAD.). Come, dance with me!

ALL. Yes, let's dance!

(*Elfin music.* ELVES *dance. See Appendix. At close enter* KING, *still dressed as* PEDDLER OF HEARTS *and carrying his full pack. He stands a moment up* C. TOAD *sees him first and runs to welcome him.*)

TOAD. The King! Ho, ho, the King!

ELVES. The King!

(*All salute* KING.)

KING. Greeting, my merry men! Here, Snatch, take my pack. (*Hands pack to* SNATCH.) Peep in there, my sly ones, and a rare sight you shall see, a fair sight—a sight those winking, blinking eyes of yours have waited many a year for!

SNATCH (*peeping into pack, then yielding it to others*). Hearts, human hearts!

KING. The hearts of Herzimwald!

ELVES (*echoing joyously*). The hearts of Herzimwald!

TOAD. Brothers, 'tis done! Our curse has come upon the town at last.

ELVES (*capering for joy*). The curse—at last!

TOAD. The gaping fools, the boasters, the smiling silly-faces! We've made them rue the day they dared to build their town so near our elfin wood!

KING. Not so fast, Toadkin; not so fast! My pack lacks yet one heart—a maiden's heart!

ELVES. A maiden's heart?

KING. You know the rhyme ——
ELVES (*chanting*).

> " Till a merry-hearted maid
> Goes alone to Elf-King's glade ! "

KING. If she should come ——
PINCH. We'll tear that silly heart out, never fear !
TOAD. It shall lie a-top of the pack, or my name's not Toadkin ! I'm off to watch for her ——

(*Turns to run off* R.)

KING. Stay ! Remember, that pure heart no elfin hand may touch against the maiden's will. All my craft I must employ to make her give it freely. Go now, my sweet one, hide in the rotten leaves, like the brown toad thou art. Watch and wait. Touch not the maid or dare to frighten her, but bring me word of her approach.
TOAD. I go ! (*Runs off* R.)
KING (*to others*). Ha, ha, it was too easy ! Think of them now, the fools of Herzimwald; their good hearts here in my pack, while our hearts, our false hearts, weigh in their breasts like lumps of stone !
ELVES. Good, good ! Rare sport !
SNATCH. I feel like dancing !
KING. Be as merry as you will.

(ELVES *dance as before* KING'S *entrance.* KING *sits on stump as on a throne, hugging the pack of hearts and watching them. Dance is interrupted by return of* TOAD.)

TOAD. She comes, she comes !
ELVES. The maid ?
KING. What ! Comes she merrily ?
TOAD. She's singing. Hark to her !

(*All listen.* GRE.'s *voice is heard singing bravely to keep up her spirits.*)

KING. Hide then, one and all. To cover ! Stir not so much as a leaf until I bid you rise.

(ELVES *hide as before* RUD.'s *entrance.*)

Enter GRE., *glancing nervously from side to side.*

GRE. (*singing*).

> Sad hearts droop along the way,
> Glad hearts dance till close of day,
> So I'll keep mine light and gay —
>   Singing, singing on my way!

KING (*affecting surprise*). Hey, the little Goose-girl! Welcome, little Goose-girl!

GRE. (*starting in fright*). Oh!

KING. What! Not afraid? Not afraid of the poor old peddler? See! (*Returns to* PED.'S *voice and manner.*) Give thy silly heart to me, here's a gayer far for thee!

(*Takes ribbon with tinsel heart from neck and approaches* GRE., *who shrinks away.*)

GRE. No, no, I know you now! You are the Elf-King. Harm enough have you done. Tears and sorrow have you brought to Herzimwald. Oh, sir, have mercy! See, I kneel to you. (*Kneels.*) Give me back the people's hearts! Let them have their happy hearts again.

KING (*with mock sadness*).

> No, ah, no, forevermore
> Sad their heavy hearts and sore!

GRE. Oh, dear, oh, dear, what shall I do? (*Rises from knees.*) I—I suppose I can just go home and try to comfort them ——

(*Turns quickly to go off* R. KING *motions to* ELVES, *who rise up and bar her way.*)

KING (*dropping* PED.'S *voice*). No, little Queen-of-the-Geese, ah no! Your light heart bides here in the forest with us.

GRE. Let me go! I must go!

(*Tries to force way past* ELVES.)

ELVES. No, no! (*They threaten her.*)

GRE. (*to* ELVES). Oh, so you think I'm afraid, do you? Well, I'm not, not very! (*To* KING.) And I'll tell you something you don't know. Rudolf the Wood-cutter bought nothing from the Peddler. These two days he has been in the forest, but he'll go whistling home at fall of night, so—so there'll be one human heart after all in Herzimwald!

KING (*solemnly*). Rudolf the Wood-cutter shall never go home!

GRE. But Rudolf is safe. You cannot hurt him. He has my primroses!

ELVES (*wincing*). Primroses!

KING. Silly child! Think you your baby charms can prevail against my mighty magic? My elves have my commands to make short work of him.

TOAD (*boastfully*). Yes, yes, we'll pluck his eyes out!

PINCH. We'll tear him limb from limb!

KING. But you shall save him, Gretel, if you will.

GRE. I? How can I?

KING (*coaxingly*). Give me your heart, your little sad heart, and Rudolf shall go free. Give me your little ugly human heart, and wear this golden one instead.

(*Advances with tinsel heart. She retreats.*)

GRE. No!

KING. What? Not to save your playfellow? Not to save Rudolf? A brave heart, yours! A loyal, loving heart!

GRE. Oh, Rudolf, Rudolf, forgive me! (*To* KING.) No, I will not listen. You shall never have my heart.

KING. One more chance, one more, before I loose my elves on you!

(*Tries to fling ribbon with heart over* GRE.'s *head. She dashes it aside.*)

GRE. No, no!

KING (*to* ELVES). Fall on her! Tear her to pieces!

(*As* ELVES *drag* GRE. *this way and that,* RUD. *enters.*)

RUD. Elves, and Gretel! (*He holds up primroses;* ELVES *howl and shrink back.*) Back, I say, back!

(ELVES *hide faces and fall back.* KING *tries to creep round behind* RUD. *who turns suddenly and thrusts primroses like a torch into his face.* KING *drops pack, howls, and runs off, followed by* ELVES.)

GRE. The hearts!

(*She snatches up the pack. As* ELVES *retreat,* RUD. *stands triumphant, one arm round* GRE., *the other holding the cross aloft.*)

CURTAIN

SCENE 2.—*Same as Act I.*

(*The* BAK., *the* C.-M., *their wives and other women sit about in idle, despondent attitudes.* BUTCH. *and* COB. *are engaged in fastening* PRINCE'S *proclamation, a large official document with red seals, to frame of booth up* C. *They move slowly and listlessly, very much as if their hearts were not in their business. The* BAK. *watches them moodily.*)

BAK. No, no, no! That's not it. A little more to the right there; no, to the left. No, that's too high. Nobody can read it there!

COB. (*dropping work to rush at* BAK. *with hammer*). Butter-face! Dough-head! Who wants to read it?

BAK. (*warding him off*). Stop! I can read it well enough to see what will happen to you, Peter Heel, if you dare strike me again! (*Stands on tiptoe and reads.*) "Proclamation of His Royal Highness, Prince of Herzimwald. Oyez, Oyez, Oyez, hearken and obey! Whereas the present bearing and conduct of the people of Herzimwald doth cause his Royal Highness great displeasure, such bearing and such conduct shall immediately be changed. Glum faces, harsh words, noisy brawling shall from this time forth be absolutely forbidden within town limits. Cheerfulness, industry, smiling countenances are absolutely commanded by order of the Law. Fines for violation of same as follows: Every sigh or groan, one penny; every harsh word, one penny; every blow——" (COB. *gives him smart blow on ear.*) Ouch! Five marks!

(*As* BAK. *dances with pain,* BURG. *enters hurriedly.*)

BURG. Stop—wait! 'Tis my business to collect the fines!

(*Produces note-book and pencil.*) Now then—Peter Heel, for brawling, five marks! (*Writes in book.*)

Cob. (*throwing his purse to* Burg.). Here. Take it, take all I have in the world and let me at him!

(*Makes dash at* Bak. *who runs to hide behind women.*)

Butch. What, I say, is this? (*Points to proclamation.*) That there's not justice. Every man has a right to be as miserable as he pleases!

Cob. (*crowding him roughly aside*). Tyranny it is! I'm for resistance. On to the Palace——

Burg. (*writing*). Hans Fleischmann, one penny. Peter Heel——

Butch. Stop, stop, or we'll all be ruined!

Burg. Ruined? Yes! And who cares, Sausage-head, who cares? The town is making money. The town, ha, ha! And the town's pockets are stitched in my breeches! (*Enter the* Prince *with* Bel. *who is pale and moves slowly as if in a dream. Several* Girls *follow her slowly with downcast heads. As* Burg. *sees* Prince, *his rough manner changes to one of fawning politeness.*) Ah, your Highness! (*Bows.*)

Prince (*seating* Bel. *on bench*). Good-day, Sir Burgomaster, and how is the new law working? An excellent idea, that, I flatter myself.

Burg. A splendid idea, a magnificent idea, your Highness—for filling my pockets!

Prince. I am being obeyed, of course? (*He comes down* C. *People turn their backs.*) Everybody busy? Everybody cheerful? A smile on every face? Eh? What? Turn this way! (*People turn reluctantly and show glum looks.*) Smile, I command you, smile!

(*People, except* Cob., *adopt horrible grins.*)

Cob. Not I, your Highness. I've paid for my misery, and miserable I will be!

Prince. This folly must be put an end to. My patience has its limits. Come, come, friend Cobbler, play the man! Forget this chatter of enchantments, shake off this melancholy dream. Merry you shall be, whether you will or no! Why, all my life I've heard of the gay songs, the romping dances of the folk of Herzimwald. (*To people.*) Come, if you won't work, you shall sing. Perhaps, by some good chance, your voices may arouse my sad love here! (*Goes to* BEL. *and kisses her hand. She does not look up or move.*) My beautiful Belrose! (*To people.*) So sing, I say, sing and dance—or 'twill be the worse for you!

COB. (*groaning*). It could hardly be that, your Highness, but if we must, we must! Come along there! (*He beckons to people who, with the exception of* BEL. *and the* BURG., *slouch unwillingly forward.*) Karl Butterbrot, you'll lead!

(*Threatens* BAK. *with an old boot.*)

BAK. (*whining*). I'll not, I say! I'll not stir a step, I——
COB. (*throwing boot*). I say you shall!
PRINCE. Peace!
BURG. (*writing*). Karl Butterbrot the Baker, one penny——
BAK. Quick, quick! I can't afford it!

(*He takes place as leader. People sing, dancing between verses of song. All wear fixed, glum expressions, and move unwillingly as if jerked by strings. In expression and movement this dance should caricature the gay romp in Act I.*)

PEOPLE (*singing*).
    Deary-me, oh, deary-me,
      Life is sad as sad can be,
    Nothing's good that I can see,
      Deary, deary, deary-me!

    Grumble, grumble, sigh and groan,
      This sad heart is not mine own,
    'Tis the Peddler's made of stone,
      So I sigh and groan!

    Tears and sorrow are my lot,
      Through the Peddler and his plot,—
    Talk of comfort I will not—
      Sorrow, sorrow is my lot!

    Deary-me, oh, deary-me,
      Life is bad as bad can be,
    Nothing's good that I can see—
      Deary, deary, deary me!

(*At end of song* PRINCE *waves hand impatiently and people bow and return to places.*)

PRINCE. I thank you. That is enough!

BAK. But we've got twenty-nine more verses, your Highness.

PRINCE. Spare me, good Baker! Your songs are worse than your silence.

BURG. (*who has been writing busily*). Not too fast, your Highness, not too fast. Our profits are mounting up. We're making money—rolling in money! (*Reads.*) Karl Butterbrot, Hans Fleischmann, Lotta ——

PEOPLE (*threatening him with any weapons handy*). Stop!

PRINCE. Will you all be quiet? Peace, I say! I'm weary of your snapping and your snarling. Oh, for that one bright face, that one little light heart the Elf-King left me! Has any one news of Gretel?

BURG. The Goose-girl? Oh, yes, your Highness, oh, deary-me, yes!

PRINCE. What? Has she returned?

BURG. She hath not, and never will.

PRINCE. You mean ——

BAK.'S WIFE. He means, your Highness, that she is in all probability dead!

PRINCE. Dead? Little Gretel dead?

BURG. (*with malicious satisfaction*). Aye, pinched to death by the wicked elves in the forest, where you sent her!

PRINCE. It can't be true!

BAK.'S WIFE. Without doubt 'tis true.

COB. Let us always try to believe the worst.

PRINCE. Little Gretel! Oh, I should never have let her go!

BAK.'S WIFE. I told you so, I told you so! Didn't I warn your Royal Highness? Magic, I said, wicked magic, but nobody would listen.

BAK. Who would listen to you? Stupid!

BAK.'S WIFE. And now 'tis too late, too late! Sorrow and sighing won't bring Gretel back again. (*Goes to* BEL. *and shakes her by arm.*) Do you hear, Belrose, Princess Belrose! You'll never see your little friend again. Gretel the Goose-girl is dead!

BEL. (*starting, and rising slowly as if awaking from dream*). Gretel! Gretel!

(*She takes an unsteady step forward, stretching arms as if to some unseen person, then falls back in* PRINCE'S *arms*.)

PRINCE. She is dying!
BURG. And the Peddler has triumphed!
PEOPLE (*groaning*). The curse! The curse!

(*As they gather about* BEL. *sound of voices and laughter heard outside.*)

PRINCE. Hush! Listen! What is that?
BURG. A strange sound! I've heard it before, somewhere—long ago!
BAK.'S WIFE (*as laughter sounds nearer and gay music begins*). Elves' music! Wicked music!

(*Holds hands over ears.*)

PRINCE. No, no, the best music in the world! Laughter—happy laughter! (RUD. *and* GRE. *run in, holding pack of hearts between them. Those* BOYS *and* GIRLS *not already on stage follow them and group in background.* RUD. *and* GRE. *drop pack at* PRINCE'S *feet, bow, and begin a merry dance down* C. *The* PRINCE, *who is up* C., *opens pack, appears to take something from it which he gives to* BURG. *who slips it into daughter's kerchief.* BEL. *instantly revives, smiles, and stretches arms to* PRINCE. BURG. *helps himself from pack and hands it to people who scramble to recover their old hearts, dropping false ones. By the time* RUD. *and* GRE.'S *dance is over, spell is broken, people have recovered their old joyous spirits, and are shaking hands, hugging one another, and dancing for joy. As* GRE. *and* RUD. *bow and retire.*) How now, my people of Herzimwald, hath every citizen his own light heart again?
PEOPLE. Yes, yes!
PRINCE. Then keep them kind and keep them good. And, henceforth,—remember. Seek only the true gold!
PEOPLE. Only the true gold, your Highness! Only the true gold!
COB. (*jumping on bench and waving boot*). Health to our Prince! Hail to our Prince and our Prince's Bride!
PEOPLE. Hail! Hail!
PRINCE. Hail to Gretel the Goose-girl and Rudolf the Wood-cutter who have saved the town!

PEOPLE. Hail! Hail! May they live long and merrily!

(*Music. See Appendix.* PRINCE *with* BEL. *stands down* L. BURG. *down* R. *Older people in background.* BOYS *and* GIRLS *drag* GRE. *and* RUD. *down* C., *take hands and dance round them, singing first verse of People's Song,* "*Ha, ha, ha, and ho, ho, ho!*")

CURTAIN

THE PEDDLER OF HEARTS

MUSIC

The melodies of the Swedish and French folk tunes can be found in the Progressive Music Series, Vol. II, published by Silver, Burdett & Co., New York. Price, by mail, 45 cents. The piano accompaniments are in a separate volume.

The German Folk Tune can be found in any collection of German folk tunes and also occurs in the opera of Hansel and Gretel by Humperdinck.

No. 1. PEOPLE'S SONG AND DANCE IN ACT I.

> Ha, ha, ha, and ho, ho, ho!
>> Life is full of sunshine, so —
> As along my way I go,
>> I must laugh, ho, ho! ho, ho! etc. (*See text.*)

German Folk Song — People's Song, No. I

NOTE. Gretel sings a verse of this song on her second entrance in Act I, Scene II, and another when she appears before elves, Act II.

No. 2. ACT I, SCENE I. DANCE OF GIRLS.

Same to be used for dance of Boys and Girls in same scene.

Dutch Dance — DITTERSDORF

THE PEDDLER OF HEARTS

No. 3. ACT I, SCENE I. ELF-MUSIC AND MELODY OF PEDDLER'S SONG.

Same to be used wherever "elf-music" is indicated in play.

PEDDLER'S SONG — "Hey, ding-a-ding, a-ding!
                 Hearts on a string, a string." — etc.

Either of two following melodies can be used.

Swedish Folk Song

French Folk Song

32 THE PEDDLER OF HEARTS

No. 4. ACT II, SCENE II. PEOPLE'S SONG, No. 2.

"Deary-me, oh deary-me!"
Same melody as People's Song, No. I, but in the minor.

Music Cues

ACT I.—*Scene 1.*

Cobbler plays People's song (" Ha, ha, ha ! ") once as curtain rises, then sings four verses. People listen till last verse, then join in and dance.

No. 1. People's song. Play six times.

No. 2. Dutch Dance. Play *ad libitum*.

Cue :—" Do you want to scare the girls? They're coming now with their garlands for the Prince's arch."

No. 3. Peddler's song. Play four times.

Cue :—" Yes, and he's singing as he comes : listen ! " Play softly till : " See, here's the fellow now ! " Enter Peddler and begins to sing.

No. 4. (Same as No. 3.) Peddler's song.

Cue :—Prince's speech—" Speak ! Do you no longer love me ? " Play very softly till curtain falls. Use a mute here.

ACT I.—*Scene 2.*

No. 5. (Same as No. 1.) People's song. Play once for Gretel's entrance.

Cue :—Prince's speech—" Is there not one happy heart in this unhappy town ? "

No. 6. (Same as No. 3.) Peddler's song. Play softly till curtain.

Cue :—Prince's speech—" I beg you to go—and save your people." Use mute here.

ACT II.—Scene 1.

No. 7. (Same as No. 3.) Peddler's song, softly as curtain rises. Break off abruptly as Rudolf begins whistling.

No. 8. Peddler's song.
Cue:—Rudolph's speech—"Afraid of elves, not I!" Music plays softly; stops abruptly as he raises primrose cross.

No. 9. (Same as No. 3.) Peddler's song, gaily and loud.
Cue:—Elves' speech—"Yes, let's dance."

No. 10. (Same.)
Cue:—Elf-King's speech—"Be as merry as you will!" Elves: "Yes, let's dance!"
Repeat elves' dance.

No. 11. (Same as No. 1.) Gretel's song, "Ha, ha, ha!"
Cue:—Toadkin's speech—"She's singing."

ACT II.—Scene 2.

No. 12. (Same as No. 1, but *in the minor*.)
Cue:—Baker's speech—"Quick, quick, I can't afford it!"

No. 13. (Same as No. 1.) People's song.
Cue:—Belrose's speech—"Gretel, Gretel!" Play very softly till Prince says—"laughter, happy laughter!" then louder as Rudolph and Gretel enter. Play twice.

No. 14. (Same as No. 1.) People's song.
Cue:—People—"Hail! Hail! May they live long and merrily." Play twice till curtain.

Dances

No set dances are prescribed for the reason that most producers will prefer to use some simple steps already familiar rather than take the time and trouble to study out new dances from a form, while the alternative of employing a folk-dancing teacher to prepare the steps and give instruction in them will often be found too expensive, though in the few instances where people do not consider either trouble or expense it will add greatly to the beauty of the effect.

The dances originally used in the play were invented by Miss Grace Smith, Folk-dancing Teacher and Superintendent of Play Grounds in West Orange, New Jersey. For the purposes of elaborate production of this play she will be willing to furnish full instructions. All correspondence on this subject should be addressed to her as above. The music in the original performance was provided by two violins behind the scenes, but a small orchestra or piano is to be preferred.

Printed by Libri Plureos GmbH in Hamburg, Germany